Wellington was alone in the kennel. He had a bone.

"Yum, yum" he said. He began to eat it.

Kevin ran to the kennel. He saw Wellington with the bone.

"Yum, yum," he said.

Wellington picked up his bone and ran away. He wanted to be alone with his bone.

Wellington sat down next to a rose bush. He began to bite his bone. "Yum, yum," he said.

Then he saw Kevin leave the kennel. Kevin was coming to see him. Oh no! Wellington dug a hole.

He put his bone in the hole. He filled up the hole. He put a stone on it. Then he sat down.

Kevin came to the rose bush. He could not see the bone. He went away to play with Jelly.

Wellington fell asleep. Kevin and Jelly crept to the rose bush. Kevin had a stone. Jelly had a stone.

Kevin and Jelly put the stones next to the rose bush.
Wellington woke up. He saw three stones.

"Oh no, ... where is my bone?" said Wellington. "Kevin and Jelly have played a joke on me."

"o-e"

hole

stone

joke

bone

rose

woke

alone

High Frequency Words

was in the he a to up and
on it away see play no went
my is said me

had ran saw with be his down
next then put came could not
three where have but wanted